PREPARING FOR AN IMPENDING DIVORCE IN MARYLAND?

Info That May Help You Deal With The Most Difficult Times Of Your Life

Michael S. Barrett, Esq.

Speakeasy Publishing
73-03 Bell Blvd, #10
Oakland Gardens, NY 11364
www.speakeasypublishinginc.com

Ordering Information:

Quantity sales. Special discounts are available on quantity purchases by corporations, associations, and others. For details, contact the publisher at the address above.

Orders by U.S. trade bookstores and wholesalers. Please contact Speakeasy Publishing: Tel: (888) 991-2766 or visit www.speakeasypublishinginc.com.

Printed in the United States of America.

Published in 2018

FOREWORD

I hold a unique place in my heart for all my fellow family law attorneys who fight the good fight on a daily basis, without compromising their integrity. I meet clients at some of the worse times/moments in their lives, as they are going through a season of turmoil. This season sometimes involves dividing time with their children, filing for bankruptcies, entering foreclosures, dealing with domestic violence, and many other situations connected with family law cases. I have dealt with battles in mediations, depositions, settlement conferences, and trials that leave unimaginable carnage and (unfortunately) children are sometimes scarred by the shrapnel from the explosions of litigation. Yet, my clients endure. After this season has passed, I enter into another contested case with its own unique set of difficulties and circumstances. This is the life of a family law litigation attorney. Unless there's a settlement, the outcomes are uncertain and our fate is left up to a human Judge clothed in a robe. Within a matter of hours (or days), life altering decisions will be made by the Bench. So my fellow practitioners...we forge forward in our quest for justice...case by case.

DEDICATION

This book is dedicated to my Heavenly Father who doesn't like to share glory.

Therefore, I leave you with the following:

Philippians 4:13

I can do all things through Christ who strengthens me.

Acknowledgements

A special thank you to Attorney Keith A. Parris, who gave me my first opportunity to practice law following law school.

A special thank you to all my clients (former and present) who entrusted my Firm with their case.

A special thank you to my family for their enduring support: the wind beneath my wings.

DISCLAIMER

This publication is intended to be used for educational purposes only. No legal advice is being given, and no attorney-client relationship is intended to be created by reading this material. The author assumes no liability for any errors or omissions or for how this book or its contents are used or interpreted or for any consequences resulting directly or indirectly from the use of this book. For legal or any other advice, please consult an experienced attorney or the appropriate expert who is aware of the specific facts of your case and is knowledgeable of the law in your jurisdiction.

The Firm, LLC
137 National Plaza,
National Harbor, MD 20745
www.thefirmllc.org
(703) 227-7157

TESTIMONIALS

"Mr. Barrett is unlike any other attorney I have EVER consulted with! After speaking with Mr. Barrett and giving him a great amount of info with respect to my very intense and dangerous separation/divorce situation, I felt an overwhelming sense of peace and knew that I was going to be ok and that there was a solution to my current issue. Mr. Barret was extremely supportive, attentive, and very concerned with my situation! I was especially fond of the fact that Mr. Barrett's motto is "I DON'T HAVE CLIENTS, I LIKE TO BUILD RELATIONSHIPS"!! That statement ALONE gave me HOPE during this extremely stressful time of my and my two children's life!! Mr. Barrett was and is very professional, kind, sincere, in EVERYTHING that he did for me, and I would and will recommend Mr. Barrett to anyone who can use his expertise during a trying, stressful time in their lives. Respectfully, and Sincerely, JP."

- A Satisfied Client

****

"Michael Barrett is a great lawyer because he responds quickly to questions from both clients and potential clients. He is available via phone, text and e-mail. He works for a flat fee and always sets the expectation of how much will his services cost and what are you getting for what you pay. He does not charge per hour which is a great advantage since being afraid of contacting your own lawyer because of the fees really sucks. He does a fantastic job at reasonable prices."

- *A Satisfied Client*

****

"I am going to say that he is knowledgeable, full of integrity and quick to respond to your inquiries! I could not have made a better decision when I chose Mr. Barrett to represent my case. I would definitely recommend him to you with a million stars if they were available. He represented my case with pure professionalism and I will definitely use his services again should the need arise."

- *Jasmine*

****

"Mike was very informative and patient with me and my case. He would ALWAYS answer my calls and return missed calls. Most importantly he educated me on process and gave a very honest opinion of things, wish I would have listened to more of his advice...lol. But overall, I was very pleased with the outcome of my case!!! I would HIGHLY recommend him to anyone whose is looking for an honest and hardworking lawyer!!!"

- Ednese

****

"Mike was committed a 100% to my case from day one. I could not have asked for better services and a more responsive attorney. From the moment I first called until my case was over, I was at ease with choice. Mike makes his clients feel valued and is very engaged and in tune with his clients' needs. His committed to his cases and very knowledgeable and easy to work and communicate with. I was very pleased with the final outcome of case and I appreciated an attorney who supported me through a very difficult time."

- Josephine B.

****

"I feel so blessed to have found a lawyer with a heart rather than someone just out for the money. Divorce is never easy however the counsel that I received from Michael made my divorce simple. While I know he has several clients, he showed compassion and made me feel as if I were the only one. Michael goes beyond the call of duty when answering emails and phone calls with quick responses. I highly recommend this firm."

- Fronia W.

****

"My lawyer all around did their part and went beyond to assure that I win my case. He took the case extremely serious and wanted nothing but the best outcome by all means. He knew exactly what to do and how to go about the situation at hand and was thorough with everything concerning the case and any information I had no knowledge of. Job well done, very pleased!"

- Jane

****

Table of Contents

About The Author

Attorney Mike Barrett has been practicing law since 2003. After nine (9) years of practice, he started his own Firm in January 2012. The Firm has a focus on injury cases, divorce, custody, child support, and domestic violence cases.

Attorney Mike Barrett has represented hundreds of clients over the years. Most of the Firm's business comes from prior clients, who return for other matters and/or refer family and friends to their doors. The Law Firm boasts an area owner, which is important because he has experience practicing law in the same place where he was raised and resided most of his life. Mike Barrett "knows" Prince George's County, Montgomery County, Charles County, Anne Arundel County, Howard County, and surrounding counties. Also, the Firm has a family feel so you WILL speak to the owner and not staff. The Firm answers their clients' calls! You don't need to search for your lawyer: a breath of fresh air in this industry.

PRACTICE AREAS

- Family Law
- Personal Injury
- Divorce
- Domestic Violence

LICENSE

- 2003, Maryland

PROFESSIONAL ASSOCIATIONS

- Member of Maryland State Bar Association
- Member of Maryland Association for Justice

EDUCATION

- J.D., University of Maryland Francis King Carey School of Law, 1999-2002
- B.A., University of Maryland - College Park, Sociology, 1994-1999

PRIOR EMPLOYMENT

- Attorney at Law Offices Keith A. Parris, 2003-2011
- Screening Unit at Montgomery County States Attorneys' Office, Summer Intern (2000)
- Administrative Assistant at United States Secret Service, 1995-1998

THE FIRM, LLC

The Firm, LLC has been providing legal assistance for family law and personal injury in the state of Maryland since 2003. We help many families deal with the heartache of divorce and child custody disputes: we help clients deal with loss of income, loss of transportation, and restriction to their life activities due to being injured in a car crash.

The Firm is a general litigation practice with years of experience: we are ready to help you deal with your case. We urge you to call and tell us about your situation and help us commence a plan of action to resolve your problem. We work with trained litigators in different locations and will try to find the location that works best for you.

If you have a divorce matter, custody matter, child support issue, domestic violence case, or you have suffered injuries due to someone's careless behavior and wish to discuss with an experienced attorney, contact us.

The Firm cannot guarantee results: no one should guarantee the outcome of any case. However, we put our clients' best interest first and will give you advice based on years of experience dealing with clients in the same, or similar situation as yours.

CHAPTER 1

ATTORNEY MICHAEL BARRETT'S EXPERIENCE IN FAMILY LAW

I became interested in practicing family law in Maryland while handling family law cases for the firm where I was employed for about eight or nine years. The firm focused on family law work, personal injury work, and criminal defense cases. These are the areas where I had most of my training. I continued with family law and personal injury (work) when I opened up my own firm in 2012. I have been practicing law since 2003.

Divorce Process in Maryland

Unbeknownst to many people, you need grounds (a reason to qualify) for divorce in Maryland. I receive many phone calls from perspective clients requesting a divorce in Maryland under irreconcilable differences grounds. As of 2018, Maryland does not recognize irreconcilable differences as a ground for divorce. We have two no fault grounds in Maryland for Absolute Divorce:

(1) separation of one year or more

(2) mutual consent of the parties—meaning the parties agree on all issues and they have no minor children together. [1]

Maryland ***does*** allow divorce under fault base grounds as well (meaning you have to prove these grounds): the most popular of these is adultery, followed by cruelty, and another is excessively vicious conduct.

---

[1] ***Please note that the requirement of having no minor children for mutual consent divorces may be removed, as of this book's published date, a bill has been passed and may go into effect at the end of 2018 which would allow couples with children a mutual consent divorce.***

Why Should a Divorcing Couple Hire Separate Attorneys?

If it's an amicable divorce and everything has been worked out, you shouldn't need to hire a lawyer. One needs to pay the filing fee to file for an Absolute Divorce or Limited Divorce, unless you request a waiver: these are rarely accepted so I suggest paying the filing fee so your petition is not held up unnecessarily. Once the other person is served, and an Answer is filed, or a Default is entered (because the spouse that was served has failed to respond). ***If uncontested,*** the Court will enter the case for a 10-minute uncontested hearing. If testimony taken is sufficient, a divorce will be granted.

It is not prudent, and maybe even unethical, to represent both sides to a divorce proceeding. Unless it's a mediation where the attorney is attempting to get the matter resolved—as a neutral third party--on behalf of both parties, one lawyer shouldn't represent both Plaintiff and Defendant in a divorce proceeding.

Do I Need a Valid Reason to File for Divorce?

The actual grounds that are listed for an absolute divorce can be found in Maryland Law Family Code

7-103. The two most commonly used grounds are mutual consent and a one-year separation. Every other ground is fault based; meaning you'll have to prove adultery, or you'll have to prove cruelty, or you'll have to prove desertion, so on and so forth.

Mandatory Period of Separation Prior to Filing for Divorce

If the parties are separated for less than a year, the result may be a limited divorce or being legally separated. If you want an absolute divorce (a complete divorce) you must be separated for one full calendar year uninterrupted. I've had people try to piece/patch time together by saying, "We were separated three months, got back together for about a month, and we've been separated 10 months…so in total we have 13 months of separation." Under that scenario the couple will <u>not</u> qualify for an absolute divorce because the separation has to be continuous and uninterrupted for at least one full calendar year to obtain (what we call) an absolute divorce in Maryland.

CHAPTER 2

PREPARING FOR AN IMPENDING DIVORCE

When preparing for an impending divorce, the best thing that I can advise is to make sure you protect the marital assets. If I represent the plaintiff and there are joint bank accounts, I don't tell my clients to dissolve or dissipate marital funds, but I would advice placing assets in a safe place so we know where all the money is, and prevent possible dissipation of the money by the other spouse. Afterwards, the Court will allocate the funds as they see fit. I like to be the one that has the assets instead of chasing and looking for money that has magically vanished. In Maryland, there is no automatic injunction, which prohibits movement of assets or taking children out of state during litigation. If I can advise anything concerning child custody, it is to make sure you protect yourself as far as the custody is concerned and ensure the other party doesn't abscond with the child.

Are There Any Benefits to Filing First for Divorce?

The first to file really makes no difference at all in Maryland. It only means that the original filing party pays the filing fee. The Court doesn't care who the plaintiff is and doesn't care who the defendant is. The reason is you can also file a claim against the other person once you have been served or notified that a case has been filed against you. If the wife or husband disagrees with the allegations, she or he can also file their own complaint (a counterclaim) against the other spouse. They become a counter-plaintiff and the spouse becomes a counter-defendant.

How Long Does a Divorce Take to Finalize?

A divorce typically takes two months (if uncontested), and can take up to a year to be finalized (if contested). By administrative rules, a divorce case should be wrapped up or completed within one calendar year from the date of filing (the try by date). Unless there is some rare extenuating circumstance, the case has to be complete in one year from the date the case is filed. I've had a couple of cases in my practice that have continued past the one-year mark but those are rare.

Reasons Someone May Seek a Post-Divorce Modification

There are usually two reasons that someone may seek a post-divorce modification. Child-related modifications (related to child support and/or child custody); meaning one party is longer satisfied that the other party should have the child, or they want more time with the child. The other request is usually for a change to ***increase*** the amount of child support received, or request a ***decrease*** in child support being paid. The other modification usually involves alimony decrease or termination.

Mediation Vs Court Process in a Divorce

Mediation in lieu of extended Court litigation in a divorce only works if you have ***reasonable*** parties. If someone is asking for a resolution that is farfetched or just not realistic, then it's unlikely the matter is going to be resolved in mediation. In Maryland we also have an increasing number of cases that are resolved in via collaborative divorce process, which is something like mediation. If the parties are at odds and it's a situation that is toxic, mediation is not going to work. Most cases settle prior to trial, which means once litigation begins the case does not proceed all the way to a Judge making the final decision. Sometimes adding attorneys to the mix helps diffuse some of the toxicity because attorneys should not be emotionally invested in the outcome of the case. Many family law cases are referred to mediation by the Court: this is true for both divorce and custody cases.

Expense wise, mediation is the best way to proceed. If you don't have parties that can speak to each other and get along in an amicable way, mediation (again) will be futile. There are times a mediator is appointed and one party claims the mediator's skewed and/or is biased. If you and your spouse (or the other parent, IF you're unmarried) has the ability to solve your divorce, custody issues, and/or child support without attorneys, it's the most affordable way to get your matter resolved. Settlements require a lot of give and take that for some parties--who are in bad relationships--don't have the inherent ability to accomplish.

CHAPTER 3

ALIMONY OR SPOUSAL SUPPORT

Paying alimony or spousal support in a divorce "should be" gender-neutral. The genesis of alimony was for husbands to pay wives when they get a divorce so the former wife was not left desolate. Historically men were the breadwinners and women were homemakers. Of course, this is not the case for many families anymore. Now everyone should have equal rights to an alimony claim. The person that pays is the one who makes substantially more money. The only way you will be granted any type of alimony (rehabilitative, indefinite, or permanent) is if the other spouse makes substantially more than you make. Aside from that, someone that is self-supportive is unlikely to get alimony. For example, I've seen cases where the incomes are double, one spouse makes a $100,000 and the other makes $200,000, and the court may (***still***) not be inclined to grant an alimony award because they don't think the disparity is unconscionable and/or that a person making $100,000.00 is not self-supportive. Unless there is a huge disparity in income, Maryland is not going to entertain any type of alimony.

For What Period of Time Does Someone Have to Be Married to Get Alimony?

You can be granted alimony for any length of marriage. However, the longer the marriage, the longer the period of alimony, and the greater the chance alimony will be awarded in the first place. You may even get into the area of permanent when you cross that 20-year mark. Every case is fact specific and unique, but for very short marriages the chances of receiving alimony are drastically reduced. It's just not something that the Court is willing to do when the requesting spouse haven't established a certain lifestyle for a long period of time. When we get into that 20-year marriage mark, then we get closer to crossing into the area of permanent or indefinite alimony.

The longer the marriage, the more inclined the family law Court is to grant an indefinite or a permanent alimony award. The family law courts pay keen attention to the party's circumstances. For example, if one spouse was a stay-at-home Mom or Dad, if one spouse has a disability and they can't work, and they're not going to be self-supportive, and circumstances of that nature, the Court may lean towards more of a permanent type basis for alimony.

When Does Alimony or Spousal Support Begin and Can I Get Support During Separation?

Yes, you can ask for emergency spousal support or emergency family maintenance during litigation, prior to the final divorce. As soon as the case is filed, you can make a request for spousal and family support once you have a hearing date. The court will award a temporary emergency amount until the final hearing if you qualify. You can get support as soon as you receive your first hearing date, but that may take 2 to 3 months. The final hearing is when you would ask for a final order or a permanent order.

How Long Will I Have to Pay Alimony or Spousal Support?

How long you will have to pay alimony or spousal support depends on the length of the marriage, but when you have been married 20 years or more, then you move into the period of the Court consideration of permanent alimony; dependent on the income of the parties and the spouse's ability to find and maintain employment (of course). Alimony always depends, again, on how huge the disparity of income is, and whether or not the requesting spouse can legitimately find work i.e. does not have a permanent disability and/or requisite skill set to obtain meaningful employment. For rehabilitative alimony requests, the Courts look at how long it may take the unemployed spouse to get the training and experience necessary to reenter the workforce. All of these reasons play a role. There is no set formula in Maryland for alimony. You can locate the list of alimony factors at Maryland Family Law Code 11-106. This Code lists all the factors that the court takes into account when deciding whether or not to award alimony; which includes who may have caused the breakup of the marriage. Again, there is no set formula for alimony, like the set formulas we have for child support. Attorneys may run alimony numbers via American Academy of Matrimonial Lawyers (AAML) or Kaufman guidelines but these guidelines are not statutory like The Maryland Child Support Guidelines. Alimony depends on many factors and is always very fact-specific.

CHAPTER 4

DETERMINING AMOUNT OF ALIMONY OR SPOUSAL SUPPORT

The biggest factor in how the amount of alimony or spousal support is determined is how much money that person who is going to be the payor makes; especially when there are children in the marriage. When there are minor children, the Court may take into consideration payment made for child support and the ability of the payor to meet their own needs (as stated in Maryland Family Law Code 11-106 (b)(9). This is to say, there is no requirement that a spouse secure second employment to be able to eat or take care of himself/herself in order to pay alimony. If the unemployed spouse is refusing to work and has the ability to work, the services of a vocational expert may be necessary to prove one's earning potential in the current employment market.

Can the Amount of Spousal Support Ever Change?

The amount of spousal support may be changed based on material change in circumstance. If there is a disability and it's indefinite, they can make it permanent. If the person receiving funds now makes substantially more money, then the other person may request that the amount be changed. Remarriage and cohabitation may also be "triggers" for modifying or terminating alimony.

Does Committing Adultery Have Any Impact on Alimony in Maryland?

When you look at the factors in determining alimony in Maryland Family Law Code 11-106, one factor is "the circumstances that contributed to the estrangement of the parties." Yes, adultery does matter, but it's not as big a factor as it once was. Adultery may matter more, however, when it comes to child custody cases. If the marriage ends because of adultery, then the Court may look more favorably at the person who hasn't committed adultery in custody cases as someone who may be more suited to be awarded custody of the child, as compared to the spouse who is technically at fault. In many cases the adultery must also be shown to affect the best interest of the child.

Be Realistic About Amount of Spousal Support or Alimony You Will Get

Clients need to be realistic about alimony! A lot of clients and perspective clients are unrealistic, about the following:

(1) their ability to receive spousal support at all

(2) how much support they will be awarded

(3) the length of time they will be receiving spousal support.

In many cases, both husband and wife are gainfully employed and they are both self-supportive. A lot of homes are two-wage earner homes, making alimony awards less common, unless there is a huge disparity in income.

CHAPTER 5

IS MARYLAND A JOINT OR COMMUNITY PROPERTY STATE?

Maryland recognizes joint or community property, in that all property acquired during the marriage are considered marital property--except for gifts to one spouse, inheritances, or property excluded via pre-nup. This holds true, regardless of who is on the title. I receive many calls from couples who are under the impression that the house, car, bank account, retirement, and other items are ***<u>their</u>*** possession(s) because their spouse does not have their name on the property: wrong! Maryland is not a title state; therefore, it does not matter if (for example) the car's title and registration is in one spouse's name only; that car ***if*** purchased during the marriage is marital property and subject to division by the Court. Of course, a car cannot be divided like money, but the Court can grant a monetary award to the spouse who is not titled on the vehicle. Now, there are situations where one spouse who was on title voluntarily decides to remove his/her name from title, and an argument can then be made that such an act was done to grant ownership rights to the spouse remaining on title, but the Court will decide that issue. Responsibility for joint debts work the same way. After saying "I do" and/or signing your marriage license, EVERYTHING you own is an OURS; not his or hers.

Factors That Affect Division of Assets in a Divorce

The biggest factor (as explained above) is ***when*** the property was purchased. There's a rebuttal presumption that debts and property acquired during the marriage is joint responsibility or jointly owned. The Court may award a 50/50 split but parties are free to present evidence as to why an equal division is unfair. For instance, there are situations where one spouse has left the marital home for a considerable period of time and is no longer contributing to the expenses: the spouse who remains in the marital home may argue that a 50/50 split of the equity is unfair in their case. The Court will listen to both sides (unless there's an agreement—of course) and render a decision.

What Happens If Someone Owns A Home Before Marriage and Then the Property Is Put into Both Names During the Marriage?

Title really doesn't matter: the money that has been used in/on the property during the marriage, as well as improvements made is what matters most. Of course, an argument can be made that adding a spouse on title was done to grant ownership rights to that spouse. However, the Court will decide that issue if there is a disagreement as to why the spouse was added. There are many couples who owned their cars and homes prior to marriage but continue to make improvements and/or payments on those items during the marriage. Once you're married, however, if there are still payments being made by either spouse, the payment is now coming from a marital source. The result is marital contributions are now being made on what started as non-marital property. Therefore, many couples who marry later in life and acquire assets before marriage request a pre-nuptial/ante-nuptial agreement to protect the assets being brought into the marriage.

Division of Pension or Retirement-Related Assets in a Divorce Case

Courts use the "Bangs/Pleasant formula" to calculate what percentage of pension and retirement funds a spouse is entitled to receive. Generally, from the date of marriage, a spouse is entitled to a share of the other spouse's retirement funds, until the date of divorce. Basically, the court uses a formula to calculate the spouse's retirement share based on the length of marriage and does not consider the time before or after the marriage. In essence, the spouse is entitled to a share of the other spouse's retirement fund based on the marital period for which retirement was being accrued.

Social security benefits are little different. Since social security is under the domain of the federal government, practitioners cannot negotiate payments. There is a ten-year marriage period that must be covered before spouse's entitlement to social security.

Can Sale of a Jointly Titled Marital Home Be Delayed in a Custody Case?

Yes. When it comes to the sale of a marital home, the party who has custody of the minor child(ren) and/or (to a lesser extent) who runs a business from the marital home may request a period of time before the house is sold so that the child or business is not abruptly uprooted. In this case, the spouse may request use and possession of the family home for a period of time; not to exceed three years. If the request is made and approved, the Court may delay the sale of a jointly titled marital home so that the minor children are raised in a stable environment. The Court is not ***giving*** the home to one spouse, but simply ensuring they do what is in the best interest of the minor child(ren) during the statutory use and possession period. After the use and possession period has expired, the spouse living in the home may either buy their former spouse out of his/her marital share of the property OR the house may be listed for sale. Here is an extremely important point: the Court may not force the sale of property that is ***not*** jointly titled. Therefore, if both spouses are not on the deed, the Court may give the spouse that is not on a title a monetary award for their share of the equity but cannot force the spouse on title to sell the house because it is not titled in both names.

CHAPTER 6

CHILD CUSTODY

There are two types of custody in Maryland. One is legal custody, which covers decision-making, and the other is physical custody or residential custody, which covers time-sharing. There are also two different types of physical custody: shared physical custody and sole physical custody.

Types of Visitation Agreements

Visitation agreements are labeled based on whether the parties share physical custody or one party has sole physical custody. The distinction is determined by child support guidelines (even if there is no child support being requested). If each parent has the child for at least 128 overnights, it becomes a shared custody visitation agreement. Custody arrangements can be fifty-fifty one week on and one week off, four nights, three nights, every other weekend, and many other different variations. There are many different types of visitation agreements, but when we look at the calendar year, there are really just two: sole custody and shared custody. The type of arrangement can be decided by settlement or by the Judge.

Could the Court Reject a Parenting Plan Agreed Upon by Both Parents?

The Court 'could' reject a parenting plan that is agreed upon by both parents, but I have never seen that happen. The Courts are in favor of parents coming to decisions in lieu of the bench making decisions about their child(ren). The Court is a stranger to both parties, and to the child(ren), and at the end of the day the Court will not know the child(ren) as well as the parents know their own children. We only have a few hours to make a good impression to the Judge and to highlight some of the concerns about the other parent. For that reason, it's highly unlikely that a Court will say no to a proposal that the parties agree is in the best interest of their child(ren).

Rules and Regulations Associated with Relocation of a Child

If a present Order applies to a situation where the parents live within close geographical proximity of each other, then there will likely be frequent contact between the child and both parents. If a parent relocates, then the visitation schedule needs to be modified. If the parties cannot agree on a modified schedule, they will have to return to Court to have the schedule modified.

Do Grandparents Have Any Parental Rights?

In Maryland, grandparents do not have parental rights; they are seen just like any other third party, which is anyone who is not the parent of the child. Therefore, being the grandparent doesn't give grandparents absolute rights to visitation. However, depending on the level of contact that the grandparents have had with the minor child, they may have certain rights. For instance, there are many instances where the grandparents have taken care of a child for extended periods of time, and then the parents return some time later (for example, eight months or a year after) attempting to take their child back and assert their parental rights."

Based on those circumstances, the Court would consider giving the third-party grandparents visitation rights (maybe even custody) because doing so would be in the best interest of the child. Everything in custody cases revolves around the standard of what is in the best interests of the child. Regardless of who the litigants are, the Court can decide that granting visitation rights to a third party is in the best interests of the child. Conover vs. Conover analyzes the four-part test that a Court will utilize to determine whether or not a third-party should be viewed as a defacto parent. If a third party fails to meet the defacto parent criteria, the court must find that exceptional circumstances exist in order to continue with a best interest analysis.

How Long Do Custody Cases Take to Resolve?

Child custody cases that are settled without discovery should take (at most) a few months to get resolved from the time of filing. Contested cases that involve litigation could take anywhere from six months to a year to get resolved. The length of time depends on the county where the case is filed. Counties with higher populations generally have a larger number of cases filed. Other factors that affect time are as follows:

(1) whether or not there is a best interest attorney appointed
(2) whether or not there is a custody evaluator involved
(3) whether or not a home study has to be done conducted
(4) whether or not mediation is ordered.

CHAPTER 7

WHEN IS A GUARDIAN AD LITEM USED IN A CUSTODY CASE?

In Maryland, a guardian ad litem is referred to as a best interest attorney (BIA). In most counties, you will have to pay in order for a BIA to be appointed to your case. All cases are fact-intensive. When a case involves children who are too young to have a say in the matter, a BIA may be appointed in order to hear the child's voice. The child's voice/perspective can only come from the child themselves or through a BIA.

What Can I Do to Improve My Chances of Winning My Custody Case?

To improve your chances of winning your custody case, I would definitely advise against engaging in any type of social media conversations about the case. I would definitely advise against any type of parental alienation or denying the other parent access to the child(ren), without having verifiable/solid and reasonable grounds pertaining to concerns about the health and/or safety of the child when the child is in the care of the other parent. In family law cases, it comes down to being reasonable in the Court. If everything is balanced, the decision will usually tip towards the parent who is the most reasonable.

I inform my clients to make sure that they are providing financial support, even if they aren't being afforded the time with the child that they would like to enjoy. I would advise the parent who is paying child support to pay a certain amount every month and to pay it in a way that is traceable, rather than with cash. It helps to say, "Even though my client wasn't getting the schedule he/she wanted, support was still paid." It's always better to perform positive acts and to shy away from negative behavior.

Under What Circumstances Can Someone Petition for A Custody Order to Be Modified?

A parent can petition for a custody order to be modified if there is relocation, or if one parent believes that the child's grades, health and/or safety are being affected negatively. There has to be a material change of circumstance that affects the child's best interest to modify an existing Order.

Why Should Someone Always Hire an Attorney for A Child Custody Case?

It is important to hire an attorney for a child custody case so that you have someone who is experienced and who has been in court many times. A lawyer who has tried (and/or settled) hundreds of cases is more experienced than someone who simply did some research on the internet before deciding to represent themselves. Now, it makes a difference if the other side doesn't have a lawyer either: this makes the playing field a bit more leveled. Even an experienced attorney can't make things grey when they're black-and-white, but it always helps in contentious cases to have an attorney who's experienced.

Hiring an attorney will also provide a buffer, to prevent the client from having to directly question the other party. It is common for questions being asked directly from one parent to the other, snow balling into a shouting match in Court: not good!

CHAPTER 8

WILL I AUTOMATICALLY GET CHILD SUPPORT IF I AM GIVEN CUSTODY?

If you are awarded custody, you will not automatically receive child support. You will have to make a request for child support by including a request for child support in your Complaint for Custody. You can also file a child support action alone, without filing for custody. Child support may be handled two ways: One way is by going through the Court, and the other is by going through the child support office. You don't necessarily need a custody case in order to have a child support case, and you can have a stand-alone custody case without requesting child support.

If Both Parents Have Shared Custody, Does Someone Have to Pay Child Support?

If both parents have shared custody, one parent may still need to pay child support, but it will depend on the gross income of the parties and the level of shared custody. Shared custody child support guideline calculation begins when each parent has the child for at least 128 overnights.

Child support is calculated in Maryland based on the child support guidelines, so it's not a number that the Judge conjures up. Since the establishment of the guidelines, we enter numbers into a formula and receive a certain amount for the order of child support. Sometimes neither party will have to pay child support, and there can always be an agreement between the parties that they will be generally charged with the support of the child when the child is in their care because it is in the best interest of the child to do so. Maryland Family Law Code 12-204 has the full child support guideline numbers.

When Does Child Support Start? Could It Start During the Separation?

Yes, child support can start during a separation, as long as one parent physically has the child with them. The "custodial" parent can request child support, and the Court will consider it. It is best to have a Custody Order from the Court in place, if one is requesting permanent support.

Can the Amount of Child Support Be Modified?

Yes, the amount of child support can be modified based on the same standards by which Custody Orders are modified. There must be a material change in the circumstances to modify child support. This may happen if there is a substantial increase or decrease of income by one or both of the parties. Support may also be modified if the costs of maintaining the child have increased or decreased. Sometimes child support is modified for a child that has aged out, or due to a child no longer needing full time childcare.

In other cases, the amount of child support may be modified if the custody arrangement changes. There are many situations in which the parent who is receiving child support no longer has the child. Sometimes a third party or the paying parent now has the child living with him/her. If that is the case, the parent could say, "I should no longer be paying child support because the child is now residing with me."

CHAPTER 9

HOW LONG DOES SOMEONE HAVE TO PAY CHILD SUPPORT?

Child support lasts until a child turns 18 years old or if they are in still in high school until age 19. However, child support is not paid once a child turns 19 years old (if still in high school), except in the case of a child who is not self-supportive and who suffers from a condition that requires them to be taken care of into adulthood.

What Happens If the Parent Obligated to Pay Child Support Fails to Do So?

If the parent who is obligated to pay child support fails to do so, the recipient of the child support can file an Order for Contempt with the Court. The Office of Child Support Enforcement may also suspend a person's license, capture their state income taxes, and utilize other remedies at their disposal.

What Are the Common Issues That You Deal with In Child Support Cases?

The most common issue I deal with when it comes to child support is filing a Petition and not knowing the location of the other parent. Also, I have many modification requests where the parent responsible for payment is no longer employed; therefore it is difficult to put an Order in place. Child support calculations may also be problematic when one or both parents are self-employed.

How Difficult It Is to Determine Best Interest of a Child in a Custody Case?

Child custody cases can be extremely complex. There is no set/fixed way to determine best interest--there are no numbers like the ones we use for child support. The determination requires credible parties, witnesses, and evidence, and it takes an attorney who is in tune with the bench and their client. Wins and losses are very difficult to measure in custody cases, because it's all about the best interests of the children. I always encourage clients to try to get these cases settled instead of letting the bench decide their child's fate.

If you don't have parties who are reasonable, then these cases will go to trial and invariably, someone will leave disappointed. It's always better to try to reach counsel on the other side or talk to the other party directly (if they're not represented) and come up with a resolution. It might not be exactly what you want or exactly what the other side wants, but it's a good middle point. That's my suggestion. It doesn't always work, but I always attempt to get the matter settled before going to a Judge or a Magistrate.

CHAPTER 10

DEFINITION OF PROPERTY IN A DIVORCE CASE

In terms of marriage, Maryland law defines property in divorce cases in one of two ways: it's either marital property or non-marital property. These are the two distinctions that a Court can draw when examining a piece of property. If it's marital then it's subject to division by the Court. If it's non-marital then it's not subject to the Court's jurisdiction and either belongs to one spouse or the other spouse.

Is Maryland a Joint or Community Property State?

In Maryland, we don't use the term "community property". We just consider things to be marital property. Anything that is purchased during the marriage is considered marital property by the Court. Inheritance and gifts to one spouse only, even if acquired during the marriage are still considered non-marital by the Court (subject to argument, of course). Everything is subject to argument but a clear/concise definition of what we consider to be marital property is any property (real and/or personal) acquired from date of marriage until date of divorce. Therefore, the biggest argument or the biggest battle is usually not over whether a property should be defined as marital or non-marital, but over how property that is agreed as marital should be divided. For instance, one spouse may argue a 50/50 split, and the other spouse believes the property should be divided 60/40, 70/30 etc. Here is a common question that I receive E-mails and phone calls on all the time: "A property is in my spouse's name only (or my name only), what happens now?" Maryland is NOT a title state. This means the property being deemed marital or non-marital is determined by

when the subject property was acquired and not whose name is on the property.

Factors That Can Affect Division of Assets and Debts in a Divorce Case

The biggest factor (again) that can affect the division of assets and debts in a divorce in Maryland is how the property was acquired and when it was acquired. When I say "how" I mean whether the property was a gift, inheritance, or purchased via typical purchase transaction. As for debt, I mean how the debt came into existence. For example, was this a credit card that one spouse used solely or was this a credit card utilized for home improvement purposes. The length of the marriage has very little (if any) bearing on whether the Court is going to consider something as the asset of one spouse over the asset of another spouse. Length and fault are of little (if any) consequence when it comes to property and debt division in Maryland.

What Happens If I Owned A Property Before Marriage and Put the Property in Both of Our Names During the Marriage?

If you owned a property before marriage and put the property in both of your names during the marriage, combined with other factors, like both spouses living in the home, then more likely than not, this non-marital home has taken on marital features because is tainted with/by marital funds making the home subject to division by the Court. A pre-nuptial or ante-nuptial agreement prior to marriage may remedy this situation.

Now, I don't want you to be confused by the abovementioned title example, because I stated earlier in the book that Maryland is NOT a title state—this is still true! Hence, it is NOT the placing of your spouse's name on a deed or car title that makes the property partially marital but how the property is treated thereafter, and the funds used on the property during the marriage. The Courts will look to see if marital funds have been used and/or improvements made on the property during the marriage; most of the time the answer is going to be yes; especially if both spouses are living in the home during the marriage. Sometimes clients will say, "But he/she didn't pay the mortgage—I did!" This may be true, however, marital funds are ALL sources of income from either spouse once you say "I do". Your paycheck is his/her paycheck and vice versa.

What If I Attained Property During the Course of Marriage Through Inheritance or Gift?

If you acquired property during the course of the marriage through inheritance or gift (to one spouse only) then by definition that property is non-marital. If the gift is to the couple then it belongs to both spouses. When you start to use marital funds on non-marital property then it becomes partially marital. It may not be a 50/50 split but it may be subject to division by the Court nonetheless. For example, if you received a car from an inheritance and the car is not running so you used $5,000 to fix the engine, or performed other type(s) of repairs, then that car has taken on marital attributes. Hence, that inheritance is now partially marital and may be subject to equitable division by the Court. Again, equitable division does not mean equal division—it means a fair division.

CHAPTER 11

HOW DOES MARYLAND LAW DEFINE DEBT IN A DIVORCE CASE?

Assume that only one spouse is responsible financially because only one spouse is obligated to pay the debt, due to the debt being in his/her name only. The Court cannot assign a debt from one spouse to the other, or place another spouse's name on the debt. For example, if a car note is only in one spouse's name, then the Court cannot place or "assign" the other person's name on the car note. If only one person's name is on the mortgage, the Court cannot place a person's name on the loan.

However, if one spouse is walking away with a lot of debt in their name only then the Court has a way of leveling the playing field or balancing things out. What the Court can do is grant one spouse a monetary award in attempts to level the playing field because the family law Court is a Court of equity. Courts may perform a calculation and award one spouse a monetary award, taking into account the fact that the other spouse is not financially responsible for a particular debt. For example, if a spouse should get $50,000 from parties joint savings account but the spouse that is entitled to the $50,000 is not financially responsible for the house payment (because the deed of trust is in one spouse's name only), then the Court may decide it is equitable/fair to reduce or remove the right to share in the distribution of the savings account; depending on how much is owed on the deed of trust. In essence, the Court has the ability to offset some entitlements to level the playing field.

Division of Debt in a Divorce Case

Generally, the division of debt is complicated because in many cases debt is "titled" to one spouse and not the other. For instance, one spouse may have several credit cards in his or her name only, and solely uses this credit card. As mentioned, the Court cannot assign debt from one spouse to another. To resolve this, the Court (if proper arguments are made) may decide that although the debt is marital (by definition) only the spouse that uses the card will be obligated OR the Court may decide that they will offset money owed that spouse as an equitable alternative to satisfy the debt. There are many ways to deal with marital debt but each case has its own unique set of facts.

Another example would be if the title to the house is in husband's name only. The other spouse is not listed on the mortgage (deed of trust), which includes a $100,000.00 loan in the husband's name only. Even though the debt is in the husband's name only, it is still marital debt. The Court notes that the wife, however, is entitled to $70,000 of her husband's retirement. In this case, the Court has an option of subtracting the amount of retirement wife is entitled to from the amount she would owe on the marital home; due to the fact husband has the entire $100,000.00 house obligation in his name only.

The Court has the ability to order monetary awards and/or make deductions to ensure an equitable division of assets and debts.

Division of Pension Accounts and Retirement Assets

Pension and other retirement assets are divided in the same way as other property. From the date of the marriage, pension and retirement accounts are subject to division by the Court. Maryland has a set formula on division of retirement. If the pension has accrued for 20 years and the parties were married for 10 years (and all 10 were during the accrual period); then 10 of those 20 years are subject to division. If the party continues to work after the divorce then the time after the divorce is not subject to division.

How Do Courts Handle Division of Debt in a Divorce in Maryland?

The Courts handle the division of debt in a divorce in Maryland by looking at whether it is marital debt or non-marital debt and whether it should be split 50/50, which is where the battle begins. It depends on what the debt is for and the spouse that incurred the debt. The Courts will examine the debt to decide why one spouse should not be obligated on a debt, even if the debt is marital. The Court may also decide that even though the other spouse should share in paying the debt, it isn't equitable to have that spouse obligated for 50% of the debt. For example, one spouse is an avid golfer and has a retail card with thousands of dollars of golf equipment owed on the card. The "innocent" spouse has zero interest in the sport and does not feel he/she should share in paying back that debt. Under these circumstances, a family law court, may decide that is unfair to have the other spouse responsible for this retail card.

Hiring an Experienced Family Law Attorney to Handle Division of Assets

The dangers of not using an experienced family law attorney when dealing with division of assets and debts in a divorce case is that examining and dividing assets and debts can be a bit tricky and somewhat convoluted for someone who doesn't handle these matters for a living, and hence would not know the right argument(s) to make.

A person needs to know what factors are taken into consideration when it comes to defining and dividing marital debt and marital property. Arguments can be made on various types of debts and properties. For example, we can make arguments as to why the equity in the house shouldn't be divided 50/50. An attorney who is trained and has made these arguments plenty of times is just more adept to handle the litigation. This may be your first divorce or your second divorce but an experienced attorney has done this hundreds of times and has a higher level of experience. The old adage says "an ounce of prevention is better than a pound of cure." I would strongly advise seeking legal Counsel at the outset to avoid mistakes and/or pitfalls. ***An attorney does not need to be hired for every case***. There are times when a consultation will do. Cases where the parties can reach an amicable agreement and are confident in their own abilities to live by a verbal agreement or preferably draft a complete property settlement agreement won't require the assistance of a lawyer. Attorneys cost money. Likewise, doctors cost money: people self diagnose their illnesses and treat themselves all the time. People represent themselves in court as well. Sometimes it works out well—sometimes it does not. Are you willing to take that chance?

Qualities to Look for In a Family Law Attorney

An experienced family law attorney should possess vital knowledge of the relevant laws of the state he/she is barred in. Each state has different laws regarding divorce, and an experienced attorney should know the rules and know how best to protect their clients' rights.

Many people don't know their rights in regards to division of property, child custody, and/or child support. It is important to know what you are entitled to and what you are not entitled to in order to make sure you enter into intelligent Agreements. Oftentimes a person will sign an Agreement and then have "buyer's remorse" because they weren't fully informed of their rights and/or responsibilities. On the other hand, many clients are willing to walk away from many entitlements, just to have a peace of mind, as their goal is to end the marriage as soon as possible and move on with their lives. It all depends on what the client is looking for: no two clients are alike.

WHAT IS THE NEXT STEP?

If you are going through a family law ordeal, please contact an attorney to discuss your matter. You don't know what you don't know until you speak with an attorney.

If you have minor children who will be affected by the divorce, consider contacting a professional to help them deal with the changes they will be facing. There are many counselors, social workers, and psychologists willing to help.

Along those lines, a good resource is a book written by my colleague Toni Gilliard:

Never Alone: A Book For Young Children And Parents During Separation And Divorce

INDEX

NOTES

Made in the USA
Monee, IL
05 November 2026

67385061R00045